EVERYTHING BEGINS IN THE BELLY

POETRY COLLECTION

DEBRA PARMLEY

Belo Dia
PUBLISHING INC

WEAVING WORDS AND DANCE INTO POEMS

"Where we do not speak a common language, we have music and dance to express emotion and passion to all people." - Debra Parmley

Debra expresses emotion and passion as a published romance novelist and poet.

Everything Begins in the Belly is a collection of poems written during her active belly dance years. Debra Parmley is first, a writer, second, a traveler of the world, and third, a dancer. These threads are woven throughout her life, in an unbreakable braid of memory. These poems are the weavings of Debra's memories and memories of the many women she danced with.

To those who dance in their hearts and in their souls

EVERYTHING BEGINS IN THE BELLY

Beginnings

Back Stage Among the Dancers

Performing

Tent Life Upon Desert Sands

Dance Partners

After the Sun Sets, Before the Final Curtain

BEGINNINGS

EVERYTHING BEGINS IN THE BELLY

Everything begins in the belly, of a woman,
before we are born to earth.
A shooting star will sprinkle stardust, across her abdomen.
If you watch her closely, her eyes will sweep,
softening, as she breathes in deep.
Tonight, nightingale sings.
Scents from the jasmine flowers far away, in another place,
shift, drift,
past the garden gate, to hover on the deck,
where wind chimes, and a yellow citronella candle, dance.
She is surrounded by her audience of flowerpots,
all summoned here to watch.
Even the red flowered trumpet vine rejoices,
rising out of the dead tree stump, roots twisting under-
ground, invasively.
The red fox will stop by the edge of the lake,
to watch her pull up energy, out of the earth,
another belly.
Now, beneath the silver moon, the woman will dance.
Long hair flowing out behind her, hips circling,

as with each flick of a wrist circle,
her fingertips fling stardust across the yard.
Her mind embraces the galaxy, while her heart
beats a three-quarter rhythm few can shimmy to.
Her belly will undulate like a waterfall,
and even the red fox will stand frozen,
forgetting how to drink.

CREATION DANCE

Dance with me, creative force -
bring me into the gift of creating,
when all the world sings with us,
as the flowers rise from their wintry homes,
as the oceans crash in as cymbals,
as the world sings, yes.

Spin me round and round again,
in the creation waltz,
till the sky spins, and the clouds dance,
as my spirit soars with the birds,
and the wind blows the whisper of a flute,
while my heart rises to be one with all.

Land me softly,
on solid ground,
for the force of creation,
is sometimes more than a body can stand,
and the spin of the dance

is stronger than some souls can take,
without falling.

Then I will catch my breath,
from the reel and spin of the dance,
to stand quiet, saying only, yes.

EARTH EGG AND MOON EGG

.

A living Earth imprisoned within a crystal egg,
clear, hard rock floating, tip top of a dark void.
Balanced in the center, surrounded by clear supporting
material,
never knowing it rotates in its own little world.
Which belly birthed this egg,
and why such a large egg for such a little Earth?

Moon imprisoned within another egg,
this one blue – is the moon blue?
Or is it the egg?
I'd be sad too,
forced to live inside that hard crystal.

Perhaps these eggs are different worlds,
dropped across the sky like Easter eggs,
scattered for little children to find.
And if so, what kind of children are out there, looking?

Written after viewing The Glass Sculptures of Christopher

Ries, "Glass and Light" at the Everhart Museum, Scranton,
PA. March 24 – June 21, 1996

Clear Flame, 1994 and Opposing Views, 1990

Ries forms illusions in large blocks of precision optical glass
that can weigh over a ton. The three-dimensional nature
allows light to move, creating images that materialize,
evolve, and vanish as the viewer moves around the form.
The glass seems to be alive.

PREGNANT

She is pregnant again, fertile as a rabbit,
the exuberant life within
always takes her by surprise,
for it is never planned, and fate laughs
at her acts of prevention.
She is pregnant with poems,
as she wakes, she feels them kicking,
restless within,
hand to belly, she repeats an old refrain –
"Hello," she says, eyes wide with surprise,
"I wasn't expecting the miracle of you."
She closes her eyes, whispering,
"I promise to love you."

HUSSY

When my great aunt visited, she told mother,
if I didn't take that nail polish off my fingers,
people would say I was a hussy.
But I was only thirteen,
and loved my pink pearl nail polish,
because it reminded me of the seashells
I collected on the beach every summer.
Other girls wore blue or green eye shadow,
but I wasn't wearing makeup yet.
My great aunt would have told them,
if the good Lord had wanted women
to have all those colors on their eyelids,
he'd have put them there himself.
In her day, pale proper ladies wore hats and gloves,
carried embroidered handkerchiefs,
to blot pursed unadorned lips.
I thought her colorless, joyless,
as she said hush, sit still, be quiet.

How voices from the past linger on,

beyond the graveyard,
and I suppose this is why, I,
will only wear a touch of lip gloss,
during the day,
and though the river sandals on my feet say comfort,
natural, nature,
my toes, which peek out like impulsive children,
say "poppy red."

Perhaps there was a hussy inside,
longing to get out,
for as a grown woman, fully in her power,
I belly dance, wearing sparkling costumes,
coins jingling on my hip scarf,
after painting on the blue or green eye glitter,
so that I might sparkle as I dance,
twirling with a laugh.

Note: Websters – Hussy 1) A lewd or brazen woman. 2) A saucy or mischievous girl.

SHOES

I wore shoes.
Stiff, chunky, corrective shoes,
unforgiving shoes with metal plates
that had no give.
My feet would ache.
Grandma rubbed rub Vicks Vapor Rub
across my arches, as she sang "Silent Night."
A lullaby.

At elementary school, the other girls
wore shiny black patent leather,
and skipped about, leaping from their toes,
I stood in heavy shoes, watching.

My gym class uniform and navy gym shoes,
made me appear to fit in.
Until I ran, tripping myself, falling,
as I tried to keep up.
Last to be picked for a softball game.

Those glamorous high heels, pointy toed
instruments of teenage torture,
made me wobble until I learned to balance.

My senior year, working at the mall shoe store,
after morning classes, I learned about fitting,
how to measure people's feet.
How some cram their feet into shoes too small,
like the step sister in Cinderella,
making their toes curl under.
Such self-inflicted pain, made me wonder
about Chinese women whose feet were broken,
and then bound, because that was considered beautiful.
Did they ever long to dance?

Flip-flops of freedom, allowed for wiggling toes,
platform shoes made me taller,
and Dr. Scholl's sandals were good for feet.
White wedding shoes walked down the aisle,
and soon,
stretchy slippers eased swollen pregnant feet.

We bought baby shoes for our first child,
while I prayed he'd be born with healthy feet.

One day I looked in the mirror and said,
"Cinderella, I regret to inform you,
there is no shoe which properly fits."
Then I stopped trying to fit in.

Wanting my children to learn to feel freedom, we walked
barefoot in the grassy yard, as they learned to walk.

My nephew would cry if you took his shoes off,
even for a nap.

Running barefoot in the soft grass with my sons,
we learned to feel the earth, sinking feet into freshly tilled
soil, where earthworms tickle.

At the beach, we wiggled our toes
down into the sand, as water swept up,
and over, and then away,
sinking down into that warm sand,
we left our own patterns.

When the children grew and went off to college,
I learned to really dance,
discovered belly dance.
A dance from deep in the soul.
In the dance studio, I smiled, as dance sisters
danced with me, in ballet shoes or barefoot,
spinning about the room, drumbeat beneath
my feet,
and the earth below pulsing.

FLICKER

The poet slides words across the page
like a violin - the bow dances,
as the words, singing, slip into your soul,
to glisten there, nestling like white stars
against a dark sky.

And do the celestial stars
then look down upon the earth,
to glimpse that poet's quick flare.
A flash so bright, perhaps they smile to see,
the poet who then replies,
as back and forth the poems do flow,
bright souls flickering in turn,
like fireflies.

PRELUDE

All the ones that come before
are merely preludes to the one that is.
Until we can no longer turn away, or if we do,
we will return over lifetimes and timelines.
Our souls simply seek what is true.
For this that is and has no name, exists
on another plane, and we are but
shadow dancers upon this stage.
Our shadows then dance upon that other plane
as if our busy lives mean something more
than moments stolen away, distractions
we insist come first, before the final act
which has no end.
This growing thirst will not be quenched,
until shadows and dancers, merge
and the truest music begins.

THE DANCERS, BACKSTAGE

CARMEN

Within you lies a light so strong,
no man could ever put it out,
while you draw breaths upon this earth.

This light, it is the brightest star,
which will shine out through the dark of pain,
and with each breath you take,
you will grow stronger.

And this is my meditation for you.
I breathe love in, and breathe it out again,
breathing nightly,
I send this love to you on the wind,
that you might breathe love in,
and hear these words and heal.

DRUMBEAT

She's done 'the right thing,' followed society
standards for so long she started to feel ill
with wanting to break free of being
the 'good girl.' Sweet, quiet, shy, going along,
never dancing to a lively song.
Enough of that getting nowhere slow.
She's ready to shake loose, so, turn the music up loud,
she'll feel the sound beneath her feet,
as she dances across the room.
Oh, and how those hips will shake.
She'll spin so fast, you'll never catch her,
as power rises within, the essence of woman.
How a man can be mesmerized,
as hip drops will capture a man's eyes.
For hours he will watch her moves,
and she will dance all night,
because she's tired of thinking,
and her limbs must move
to keep from quaking.
He likes those shoulder shimmies too,

because the girls are dancing; it's a wonder
they don't bust loose.
There's not a man here she would choose,
and no, he can't come home with her,
no matter how he pleads.
She's there to dance and wants her freedom.
It's safe enough with her belly dance sisters,
those Goddesses will keep her safe
from everyone but herself.
She's dancing with her shoes off now,
the rugged beat beneath her feet,
rising to touch her heart, beating within,
like some pagan girls,
who've never heard of sin.
Her passion flares beneath the night sky,
and it must go somewhere,
so, she will flare, lighting up the darkness,
her life song singing,
one more flare,
before the music dies.

SHADOW ON THE WALL

The moment she answers the phone, her face changes.
The smile falls, like a mask dropped to the floor,
and while she speaks not a word
her body says she will do as he says.
and we can only guess at what is being said,
on the other end of that line.
Then she is gone
suddenly
without one word goodbye.

And this is how quick life can be snuffed out.
Quicker than this breath I hold,
these eyes which close, for this dancer I know -
shadow of a lost soul,
her silhouette lingering, against these walls
long after the door closes,
the shadow dancing on without her,
like a candle which flickers -
And she will not be made whole,

until she learns to say no,
and the winds of inner change
begin to blow.

BEAUTIFUL OBSESSION

You are my beautiful obsession,"
he says, "and I can't stay away."
He runs his fingers thorough her slippery hair,
murmurers "like silk."
She feels hot breath upon her neck,
he runs one finger down her spine,
making every nerve come alive.
"Don't move," he says, his hands run down,
to palm her cheeks. "What is it about you?"
She doesn't reply,
and has no answer for what is, or isn't true,
that he would listen to.

"You are so hot," he says, "You are my beautiful
obsession." He repeats.
"I can't stay away from you."

She closes her eyes,
wondering if he has ever tried.
There was a time when his words and touch,

wooed so smooth she would sigh with delight,
as he danced her around the room.
But now she knows the only truth of his words.
She is his beautiful obsession,
that much is true.
That fairytale dance has ended,
now that the light is turned on.
Once upon a time, she longed to be
his beautiful beloved,
and how his words could woo,
as she heard her dream coming true.
His words now only woo himself,
as he squeezes her for everything
his dream refuses to awaken from.
And she can no longer stay still, or silent.
With open eyes, all fantasies must fade.
Him not being who she thought he was.
When she speaks and moves, he stops
and frowns, watching his beautiful obsession
distort
into a moving, speaking, real woman.

FADED FRIEND

I tell you, my dear, you have nearly faded away,
are almost a ghost, but I still see you,
and hear your heart, which longs to dance.
You were quite simply, a fool, in love
with a man, a destroyer of dreams.
Yet you destroyed your own dreams,
by negating yourself for a chance
at happy ever after, romantically believing
good girls always become the beautiful princess,
and win,
because a prince comes charging in.
In full pursuit of you, he charged
with sweet whiskey kisses, which spun you
on your head, until he wanted to change you
and the fading did begin.
At first you let friendships grow distance,
because you always had a date,
he had no interest in your friends,
and then after you married,
we never saw you again.

Were you forbidden? You were never alone.
The tag along insisted interest; in everything
you did. But he did not care for dance sisters,
finding something wrong with each,
something you did not defend.
He would whisk you away, on his horse,
to live in a cave, or a castle deep with moat,
a drawbridge and his desire,
to keep everyone away.
Did you feel the fading start, see yourself
in the mirror, did you dance in silent rooms,
before he entered, or avoid mirrors,
forgetting how you looked before,
while he told you how radiant you are,
even as you faded, for him,
your dancing feet no longer taking you outside.
Come take my hand, I see your inner dancer.
And we shall dance once again.
I'll put music on that you loved, a mirror dance, and if you
look into my eyes, dancer to dancer,
I shall help you come into solidity again.

BARBIE SPEAKS

He loves the idea of her,
of what he molded her into.
Blonder, smoother, hotter, wilder,
nothing is ever perfect enough, for him.
Though quiet, because she has mastered the art
of being still as a stone,
inside she is quite alive.
She has become numb, dumb, off in dreams,
somewhere far beyond any man's touch –
and he doesn't see her any more,
but perhaps he never did.
The woman inside who is fully alive finally
decided to speak up.

Facing the woman she now shows to him,
he shakes his head, says no, it isn't true,
asks her when she changed.
She's been changing since the day they met,
to suit his moods.
Somehow she didn't know

her life was entirely hers to choose-
she who does not vote or voice,
gives up her rights, the loss her choice -
something the shy find entirely too easy to do.
And he of all people should know
what it is to not fit into a mold.
Black sheep he calls himself, because he never fit
into his family's mold.
How is it then he needed her to fit into one?
From the smallest of things,
which plates she uses, which foods she cooks,
or whether she watches his T.V. shows –
he loves the idea of her,
the woman he molded her into.
He doesn't see the woman she is, perhaps
he never did.
Perhaps he wanted a twin. One to mirror
what he does, and says, for two can't be wrong -
which validates every choice he makes.
But she can no longer bear to be so led
in everything she does.
She has thought hard, on whether her choices
come from the true woman inside,
or if they are things she has been trained to.
She began a list.
She does not like sports, though long ago
she cheered for him. Her pom pom's are gone
and football makes her want to leave the room.
Yet she is not inactive, and loves to dance
so much, that she will dance alone,
away from her belly dance sisters,
when he is not at home.
She will not stop dancing,

just because he wants her to,
for it's something that lives deep within her,
something deep and true.
He cannot have the wife he wants,
that woman does not exist,
and she will no longer be so blonde, so quiet,
so still. Something has grown inside of her
until
it longs to be free of molds,
of arms that hold too tight,
of what is loud and forceful
and insists on being right.
And this is but one thing on her list.
He was right to be concerned,
for Barbie has found
her new dancing shoes.

YOUR GIFT

What joy
to simply know
that you exist
to gift the world
with the song of your smile,
and all that arises from deep inside -
such a gift
that only you
can bless this world with.
And even if others cannot see
the light that lives
inside of you,
I do,
And it is enough,
to make one soul
dance in bliss.

SLEEPING BEAUTY SLEEPS

Sleeping beauty doesn't want to wake,
because her current life,
is more than she can take,
and in her sleep she is free to dance,
for there is not a chance
the beast can follow her there,
and she does not have to beware,
of men who would cause her pain,
for she is free of all the chains
which bind her to the life she lives,
and she is simply free to give
the love in her heart which wells within,
as she dances and spins.

TRIBAL ROARS

What do you see inside
when you come undone...
and what do others see...

One night I spun around the dance studio, eye to eye with
Asha, troupe director, because
she'd chosen me, and said "let's show them,
how to mirror, tribal style"-
we began to dance, eyes locked, circling
in tribal movements-
we spun around the room, in sync, faster
and faster, shimmying with snake arms,
until the room ran with color, and she said, 'Stop. I know
you are dizzy.'

I have that quiet roar within, the inner drive
of the tiger,
so low, few but me can hear it.

Somehow, she sensed I'd spin

until I lost all control,
and something in me fed upon each breath
that took us closer to that point in time.
I would not have stopped at the edge
of anything.
This I know.

The dancers' eyes were wide,
I don't know what they saw, inside my eyes,
how two dancers communicate with only eyes
moving in sync.

I suspect she glimpsed inside,
where my white tiger resides.

Sometimes there is a wildness in me.
An untamed tiger, which waits quietly.

At eighteen when my tiger roared, I walked out,
moving into the wild unknown.
Then being on my own, I had to keep that kitty
inside, under control -

Asha and I danced around the bonfire,
celebrating summer solstice.
She watches me now, differently.
She spoke of her inner Phoenix, of burning
and being reborn, which lit something
inside of me – A Phoenix slowly rising,
while my white tiger was asleep.

Oh, dare I tell you of the horrible thing
I have done -

what will come of this dangerous destruction -
I do not know. I know only this -
a Phoenix once ignited, should never touch
anything, never be allowed to burn a thing,
except herself.

I should have left them alone,
all my older poems - are gone, gone, gone.
There is no record left of any,
save the published ones,
which provided me with copies only,
and no checks -
Oh, I should never have read the older poems
at such a time, struck blind by Phoenix fire.
How naive I have been, writing on one side,
of a veil which now ripped away,
causes painful clarity I could not bear,
along with that inner flame flaring,
into a towering fire.
I destroyed them one by one,
throwing them into the fire -
until my inner tiger woke, and said, 'Enough!'
Stopping, I then sat and wrote that poem,
until spent, I fell into bed.
This morning I woke to ashes
and that whiff of smoke that tells you
something is dead.
And what will arise now I do not know.
I do not know when I shall dance again,
and cannot speak of this further,
as I am mourning poems.

PALM READER

Our palm lines are usually not fixed.
Unlike our solid bones, the lines may change,
with time, a purposeful or accidental rearrange.
What then can the palm reader tell?
Could she know the moment you fell, in love,
or the moment you fell ill.
You might have a happy marriage,
or multiple divorces, perfect health,
monetary wealth, good fortune, or bad.
My hands don't want to rhyme,
or fit between plot lines,
yet this poem keeps trying,
like a lifeline pulling back,
toward a rhyme of organized time.
But time cannot be organized,
because it freely flies, toward something
undefined by a palm line.
It's in the fullest moments, when we realize,
only after they're gone, that therein

lies the magic of destiny.
Oh, put on a song, and let's just dance,
forgetting predictions and lines.
The only time being tapped by feet
upon the floor, or fingers dancing in the air.

SHAKE AND SHIMMY

Sometimes I get a little shaky,
and don't know where I stand,
when everything around me
is preying on what stability I have.
So, I try to keep moving, travel near and far,
and when I am home, I shimmy, fast enough
to avoid what I don't know.
Oh, you won't see me quiver and quake,
cause I'm never standing still,
for when I do, the ground trembles,
as the future is moving near,
while I stand wavering, with what I should do.
There is no equilibrium here,
for it could never be so, when there is no private
place of quiet and rest
in which to be comforted and grow.
Yet I am not the shaker, constantly
stirring things up, because I can't live
without drama,
because nothing is ever enough.

And please don't chide me for staying,
while everything falls apart,
until you have stood in this spot.
Yet the more I keep on moving,
the greater this longing grows,
to cling to something sturdy,
which would anchor me,
one steady, unshakable rock.

SILENT SYMPHONY

The symphony exists inside her body,
though the conductor is away.
How can it be that this song,
heard once, in a dream,
keeps on singing.
Oh, do not ask her to write it down for you –
She never learned to read music –
She only saw black flags,
and golf clubs leaping about the page,
and longed to dance.
And do not ask her to hum this song.
Listen to her heart.
If you cannot hear it thrumming,
then you are not the conductor
the symphony awaits.

THE HEART SOARS

The heart soars, or suffers in silence.
It pays no heed to logical reasoning,
or morality.
It simply feels, and goes on feeling,
whether we acknowledge it or not.
It is big enough for pain, love, and joy,
simultaneously
and sings alone in a crowd,
where only one can hear,
or across a thousand desert miles,
where only the wind whispers in answer.
The heart will not be silenced.
It beats inside a muffled cage,
and only the brave will let it out, to dance.
For if it dances, there is no choice
but to take its hand,
and the reel of the dance
may be more than any but the strongest
will survive.

Those who are not so strong,
guard the cage shivering, in fever,
muffling its cries projecting nothing to the world
but mute silence.

SUMMER SOLSTICE MEDITATION

The bonfire flames dance, but not I - I meditate,
gazing in.
Summer solstice brings in the mid-summer,
with dancing flames, causing me to still,
thinking of how I am often too much in motion,
dancing into a spin,
or pouring words across the page,
or thinking of a hundred things.
Jane says, I am the busiest woman she knows,
and like a bee, I buzz about, the Gemini in me
allowing me to do two things at once,
while reveling in it –
but even the sun stands still sometimes.
Ancient lovers at solstice bonfires would leap
through the flames – what a leap that is.
The chance of burning.
Tonight, I look back at where I've been.
Doing is not the same as being.
To learn how and who to be, we must sit
quietly.

But who can light bonfires - only the lucky few
if city codes allow it. We the lucky few, sit
encircled by ancient trees filled with sounds
of the night creatures, and near a crackling fire.
I stare into the fire, thinking, of what was,
what is, and what is to come, and how
I don't know where anything is headed,
beyond being my authentic self.
Perhaps it's just as well, for knowing
leads to planning and more busyness.
My past tendency has been to worry,
the downside of the "what if" of a writer.
Any restlessness I feel is paused, this night.
My eyes are drawn to the flames which
mesmerize, and how I dance sometimes,
like those flames - on the edge of out of control.
But tonight, I am not filled with an urge
to dance. How strange, for I dance every day.
Tonight, I vow to take time for simple pleasures,
to be gentler with myself and others,
to learn to live in the quiet joy of the soul,
which can go with me wherever I go.

CHAMBER SECRETS

There is a chamber of this cave,
which is her body, that nobody can find:
darkened, empty cathedral, walls echoing
with the unsung.
If she closes her eyes she can feel these walls
humming a tune she doesn't know how to play,
like some Gregorian chant,
which reaches into the depths of her being.
And there are no words for this,
that she might explain it to you.
For this song has yet to be sung,
and her lips do not know the tune,
yet when she closes her eyes at night,
she feels the walls softly thrumming,
and dreams of the song gently being sung.

LIFT OFF

Some people run red lights
when no one is looking. Some will take a chance on yellow.
And some spend their whole lives, waiting for the light to
change green.
To live in that place was a perpetual hiding.
Why even the kitchen timer going off,
would make her jump.
She never learned the art of waiting.
She thought there must be some trick
she'd missed, like how to count down,
before the dynamite blew everything to rubble.
Some days she wondered
if there was anyone else like her.
In her dreams, she was lighter than air,
like when she was a little girl,
and wanted to be a fairy princess,
so she could fly away, up into the clouds
to dance.
But little girls always grow up,
and she stopped checking the mirror for wings.

Just to be on the safe side,
she never asked for anything,
that way she couldn't be disappointed.
Which is why she never had to figure out
what she really wanted.
One day she simply lifted off, sprouted wings,
and flew so high...
From the moment they met... she kept her eyes
closed, and held tightly to his hands,
for she was afraid of heights.
She kept them closed all the way down, until
she felt the earth again, beneath her feet.
"I had no idea we would be so close, so fast,"
she whispered.
His fingers, threaded through hers, squeezed.
Perhaps he thought this would comfort her.
But after flying, she was simply carried away,
by the proximity of touch.
"Open your eyes," he whispered.
The moment she opened them to gaze into his,
she felt herself falling again,
and wondered why she also felt so light.

PERFORMING

UNDER THE PULL OF THE MOON

And are you then as lonely
under the pale moon as I,
and do you hear that silver queen whispering,
in the night sky, to oceans pulled
with one brief breath she holds,
as dancing in attendance, lonely lovers fold
under as waves which crash into a dark sea,
and do you think of me.
Tumbling under, drenched I fall,
and what pull of the moon has called,
causing two hearts to beat such strong
rhythms of longing.
Dance, she commands,
imperial in the night sky.
As commanded, I spin, pirouette, fly,
across silver-blue shaded blades of grass,
with each spin, flinging away remnants
of the past.
Dizzy, with wondering what you feel for me,
and where you are within that deep sea.

Dare I trust this moon, and you,
or should I believe what Yeats felt was true,
the moon so crazed, a delicious dream
which will rend what is tender,
leaving me alone to stand,
naked as a child, reaching for your hand.
And who commands what happens
beyond now,
I ask Her Imperial Highness
who merely lifts her brow.
The crickets in the yard cry.
She will not speak to mortals such as I.

MARQUEE

Secrets she kept to herself, were never
what held her together.
No, despite all appearances, it was never more
than a stage prop. Accidentally kick one board,
it was likely to come tumbling down.
The audience is oblivious, as her beauty shines
under stage lights. If you add the right gel,
she positively glows, and they always comment
on her smile.
Behind the scenes, her shadow scurries,
mending one crack or another.
There's never enough time for more than
a quick patch, holding splinters together,
hiding truths she runs from.
When she glimpses him in the audience,
she stands frozen,
fearing truth will tear her apart.
Foolish woman, you're already splintered,
and he is not so easily fooled
by those pretty lines your audience expects

to hear.
You stand under a spotlight only he can see,
and he would notice the strain, hear the tone
in your voice, see beyond pretty eyes.
Though he cannot read your mind, he sees you
all too clearly.
Should you trust him now,
to share your doubts and fears
of how you cannot lean heavily in any direction
for fear of falling –
he stands steadily, watching, and waits
to catch your tears.
And if the stage crumbles beneath you,
he might catch you as you fall.
Yes, this is a risk, and you might fall anyway,
for there are no guarantees.
The orchestra pauses,
and you have but one moment in time,
before the next line will force you to continue.
The unlimited run of this play
will bind you here, for as long
as you lend your name to the marquee.

IN CHARACTER

In someone else's story,
you'd only be a character,
forced into some crazy subplot,
that doesn't take you where you want to go.
And it won't matter,
how much you argue with them,
for they won't listen.
And if you're not careful,
you could end up stuck,
repeating endless dialog,
or some piece of purple prose
that keeps on repeating,
like a commercial jingle you can't stand,
but can't get out of your head.
And the play runs on forever,
the run unlimited,
because there's always someone
who wants to watch you run
through the motions, so, they can reassure
themselves,

it's what you wanted,
though no one ever consulted you -
you are just a person who fits into the costume,
and you have the look for it, so of course
you must like it –
be careful then, for it is said, some ghosts
haunt this theater, long after they are dead.

MARIONETTE

The strings which pull her, are invisible
to most.
But you see past her wooden limbs,
which animated nightly on that stage,
delight her current audience.
The puppet master, she must please,
on command, never straying far
from ties that bind feet and hands
held taut with tight wires.
Yet he prevents a fall, which would break her,
and will control events,
so she will keep performing,
while her heart beats fast inside.
Such a pretty wooden figure,
her beautiful smile masking pain,
and none would guess thoughts
running through her mind, about this tied life.
She dances, yet never sings,
for she can only sing from a place of joy, inside,
and it isn't on the play bill, because

no one here knows how to play a happy tune.
This marionette dreams, of gentle hands
which kindly take the broken strings away.
Such touching movements slow and sure,
will coax her limbs,
until she then begins to sing anew.

ENCIRCLED

Circled, watched, always looked over,
looked after.
The pattern across the ground as worn as
the cheetah's path inside the zoo.
Bare dirt, for nothing can grow,
beneath such determined feet,
so nothing ever changes.
Moving inside that circle is a dance of a sort.
Solitary dancer, don't forget to smile,
everyone is watching.
Spin across the surfaces, careful now,
avoid eye contact, letting anyone see inside.
You've food and water, and no one can get in.
Why then sit on that dirt all alone, thinking,
as you live within the safety, encircled in,
the predictable caging staging of a life.

THE BELLY DANCER AND THE
EARL OF WHO

When he first saw her, she smiled back at him,
and he thought, this will be fun,
and was anxious to begin.
The excitement of what might happen next,
led him on, the eternal mystery
of a new woman
always lured him like a siren's song.

The belly dancer, unknowing, simply smiled
and caught her breath,
as strong chemistry between them, so alive,
and his shining eyes took her by surprise.
She danced, her silken veil soaring
through the air, she spun, caught up in dance,
unaware of the Earl of Who's expression
as he watched,
while he longed to touch her silky hair.

Attentive, he gave her all the attention
at his command,

and their unseen dance began.
Stunned and stunning, she followed his lead,
as he wooed, unaware of a game being played,
or of any need of rules,
for she had never been a player,
and her heart was naïve and true,
but still she was caught up
in the dream of him, the Earl of Who.

One day, he suddenly changed his name,
said he needed a break, an the abrupt stop
of their dance left her head in a spin,
as she felt a strong dizziness creeping in.
Sinking onto the floor to ground herself,
A song now echoed in her head.
Real, or real gone, the song said.
The Earl of Who was different now,
so, who had he really been?
Around this time, she gave up
on handsome, charming men.

She dances now, behind thick castle walls,
wanting no audience, lover, or man to call.
Within a pink rose bush lined courtyard,
her silken veils rise and fall,
to the rhythms of the drums,
and she has learned to spin again, and this time
not to fall.
You will not catch a glimpse of her,
through the heavy castle walls, the safest place
to express her heart, her love,
while guardian angels with swords of light
now stand sentinel, guarding her loving heart,

they permit no trespass,
there's nothing any man can do,
for the way is now heavily barred against
any man who is not who,
any man who is not true.

VISITATION

She wakes, one arm flung straight up,
over her head,
palm open, reaching for the sky,
as her other hand cups her cheek, each
a belly dance move.
She dances even in her sleep now.
Her cheek is soft and warm, and silky hair
tickles her palm, curling around
like the tickle in her mind which asks
what the dream was, which had fled.
It's three a.m.
Prime time for ghostly visitations,
or so a psychic once said.
Her heart thrums a beat she does not recognize,
as one she's ever danced to,
a chill in the air comes through the open window,
as she curls onto her side, wide awake now.
In the dark and silent room, she ponders,
who she might have been dancing for
and what it might mean,

beyond a dream.
Answers and sleep are far from coming,
as her mind is uneasy with rationalities
which do not match the beat,
of her heart now softly thrumming.

TENT LIFE UPON DESERT SANDS

INTO THE DESERT

I left the land of For Better and entered
the land of For Worse,
followed you into the desert
where nothing seems to live.
The sun beat down, scorching away dreams,
though I kept hope in a flask, close to the hip,
because I can't live without it,
and suspected you might need it too.
You brought nothing but yourself, and anger.
Those heroes of yours, John Wayne, and Clint,
always ride away alone.
But the tale is never told,
of what happens after,
and shouldn't they deserve a woman
who will mount that horse, to ride after them -
Their women always want a picket fence,
and for the hero to be something he is not.

I'd go anywhere in the world with you, for love,

with the hope that love is enough
to keep us alive.
Trudging through the sand, always behind you
because you wouldn't hold my hand,
and didn't want me there,
preferring to die alone.
I kept my eyes open, for the vista,
the view of an oasis, and dragged you,
when you refused to move,
promising water soon.
You were oh, so heavy. It took everything I had,
to move even one inch,
and when we reached one mirage
after another, I always kept hope
for the next one,
though you would never take a sip.
The day we reached one that was real,
your anger coiled inside its basket.
I, this belly dancer who closes her eyes
to slithering snakes on the movie screen,
learned to watch that basket closely,
while dancing with harem sisters,
who offered love.
That snake coiled within, ever ready
to raise its head and strike.
Foolishly, I thought to tame the beast,
If only I shimmied fast enough,
for isn't a belly dancer a snake charmer -
The trick I learned, is never to dance too close,
for even hope won't ease the pain
fangs leave behind,
and tolerance to venom, once built up,

leaves a kind of poison inside,
requiring a knife and pressure to pull it out.
How long it lingers in the body, is a question
I can't answer -
Only the sands of time will tell.

SPINNING JENNY

How to love a Jenny:
Speak softly. Whisper to her in the night,
or play the song very low,
that only her heart may hear it.
And when she dances away, spinning so fast
she runs out of your line of vision,
don't give up –
Oh, but if you love her, you never could anyway
– for love never does.
You may ask yourself why she spins so fast, dances so hard,
and though she would tell you
she doesn't know,
we suspect she runs from something long ago.
Spinning fast, she flings aside old things
that cling, as sweat rolls down her back,
dislodging memories, which linger
in the hidden places of the body.
Even so, every dancer knows
to rest between dances, stretching,
breathing deep,

and if you send her your love, as a whisper
on the wind, she will breathe it in,
and know the quenching of a great thirst.
In time, she will learn to turn,
in your direction,
looking back over her shoulder as she spins.
Every spinning dancer needs to focus,
on one spot, to keep her balance,
and will search for the strongest focal point,
eyes ever searching as she spins.
You must be willing to stand still and strong,
for a spinning Jenny can only rely
on one who is steady.
She will have found others missing,
when she spun round quick, then had to focus,
elsewhere, lest she become dizzy
losing her balance.
She will have fallen before,
learned where blind trust leads,
even more determined
to keep balancing on that floor.
Yet there is nothing a Jenny needs, or desires,
more than air, water, and solid earth
beneath her feet, along with your steadily
burning fire.
Remember to speak softly,
for a Jenny has the most tender ears,
and is easily broken –
she won't stop spinning for a hard landing.
Build the bed soft,
cover it with silken pillows.

HAREM GIRL

The dancer spins, hips swirling,
fingertips brush the air
which floats the silk veil.
She stops to face the crowd.
Her right hip lifts and drops, before circling.
She sways right, left, turns,
peers over her shoulder.
Her eyes meet his, as he pauses
amid a conversation,
watching each sensuous move,
and her senses come alive,
which heightens the glow,
begun behind the curtain
the moment she felt his presence.
Oh, yes, she felt him there, waiting,
before she took one step
from behind the curtain,
this knowledge bringing that slow smile
they always say is so mysterious.
You might think they are lovers,

yet he only sees her through the veil,
as she dances in circles, around him,
and what she will not say.
They never speak out loud,
for the room is full of music,
as people talk, laugh, gossip.
He never looks away from her
as he speaks to them,
and though he watches other dancers,
and will not say she is his favorite,
he always returns and waits
for her to notice him.

If you are expecting a tale of the Arabian Night,
him carrying her off into the desert
like a desperate man,
you would be disappointed,
for he does not seek to own her,
would not cover her from head to toe
in black cloth, or tell her not to dance.
He would not think to ask her to stop, for him,
and loves the freedom of her spirit,
the way the dance comes alive in her,
as he sees the passion within.
The moment she sees him, her heart sings,
as she feels him in her blood,
which rises in the heat of the dance,
where she pours all the passion stored inside,
each move speaking the language of love.

THE SHEIKH

(from Shekh, Morocco – "one who possesses knowledge")

If his patience was endless as the sands
which stretched across that arid land,
her heart was no less fertile, like the lush green
of their oasis where beauty flourished,
and though others might claim it merely
a mirage,
those practical friends would never travel
deep enough into the dark night
to discover truth.
So, they remained secluded.
She thought of this place as their hideaway
from the world,
this refuge safe enough to bare herself
as poisonous secrets poured out
across the pages, each line a bit easier
as the sheik simply waited,
watched and listened, while exuding strength,

and a courage to match her own.
Perhaps he remembered what it was
to bleed poison, the toll it took, or, nomadic,
he may have known other deserts,
as his words hinted at many traveled roads,
yet she sensed he would stay by her side,
this knowledge calming busy thoughts,
anxious mind, until quiet in her mind
she stopped questioning the future,
for no question could ever sound the depths
of a heart,
and no word, or promise would hold a nomad.
She accepted what was and what would be, trusted what
she knew of him to be true,
beyond the things he would say
to the things he would do.
For many men use pretty words to lure,
impulse leading only to the affaire flaring,
like a shooting star in the night, brilliant,
exciting,
only to burn out into darkness.
And this was not her way -
the oil lamp flickers in the dark tent,
steady as the whisper on the wind which says,
this is.
The thing she feels but does not name, because
she loves too deeply.
The ink at last runs clear. She runs her finger
across the empty page, the now finally reached
beyond pain and sorrow.
The realization all has been poured out
makes her close her eyes,
the future now theirs to write.

She breathes in deep, and smiling,
steps outside beyond the tent, to gaze
into the midnight sky at stars clear and
bright as tomorrow.
And this is what she wishes for,
upon the falling star –
a steady love which never fades,
and if the small star
just beyond the tallest palm tree
seems to twinkle, saying yes, this is,
she keeps this mystery to herself,
returning to his tent to bathe in scented water,
slowly savoring each movement, she washes,
sinks, rises again, breathes deeply,
and there is time to dry off, to paint the henna
in tiny floral lines across her body,
wishing to be beautiful for him, the intricacies
a secret for him to discover,
now hidden by the silk of her robe.
The moment he steps into the tent she turns,
suddenly shy and blushes, glancing down,
and when she dares look up, he stands gazing
with the kindest eyes upon her and a smile,
drinking in the sight of her.
As she catches her breath, he steps forward,
reaching for her hand,
and everything in his gaze tells her,
she's everything he'd dreamed of and more.
Emboldened she reaches out to him.
Their fingers thread together.
Butterflies' flit in her stomach
as he pulls her near,
lightheaded, knowing he will kiss her,

her breath catches as her lips part.
Then his lips brush hers gently, the kiss tender
and light as a breeze, her heart thrumming,
their lips humming, their first kiss
sweet as the first strawberry of summer.

HALF MEASURES

In the slippery dark, he moves his tongue,
like sadness across her skin, and she knows
how even the slightest kiss,
connects unfailingly to the wounded
whose heart begs to be loved.
And this is what we learn of love,
in half measures.
Loss lodging deep within, the pain of yearning,
while the body, speaking in tongues, waits
for an interpreter, crying out a lost language,
as sweating limbs position and reposition
again.
Impatient, we dance out of tune, stumbling
like those who've drunk too much,
while innocence and grace hide
beneath the skin, wallflowers uninvited
to this dance.

VEILED EYES

They never see her hair beneath the silken veil,
won't know how slippery those tresses feel,
the length or weight or color of her hair,
how tight the ribbons tied about her head,
to prevent any sort of slide into her audience,
as her hair does not like to hide or be confined.
Some women say it's safer behind the veil,
yet men will always comment on her eyes,
and more than one has viewed her as a prize,
to be taken at his whim.
Oh, do not put your trust in veils, or such men,
for that protection could be much too thin.
A woman must be wise to see past the veil,
and it is she who must gaze deeply
into his eyes,
to see beyond veils, illusions, and lies.

BRAILLE

The young fall in love by touch
and perhaps this is the reason,
such pairings break apart,
for in touching,
we sometimes listen less,
or listen, but only hear,
the sound of flesh.

DISROBING

She disrobed, too quickly.
Her clothes puddle on the floor,
languor runs through every cell,
perhaps fueled by wine,
or the light in his eyes,
which says he finds her beautiful,
something she now feels, deep inside.
She stands exposed, in candlelight's soft glow,
and he, being visual, as men are,
is so far ahead of her, she may never catch up,
not having felt the brush of his finger,
even once.
Foolish girl, why did you rush?
Oh, he said he loved you.
Well, those are the magic words, aren't they -
Abracadabra, and like a snap of the fingers,
you give up treasure, without thinking.

FEVER

She burns, feverish in her sleep,
her hand reaches out for him,
from beneath cotton sheets –
he will thread his fingers through hers,
reassuring that he is here, and it is safe to sleep.
He places a cool cloth across her fevered brow,
whispering tender words of love,
he tends her tired body, soothes her tired mind,
which dreams fitfully now,
a broken sleep
the only kind the illness will allow.
Does she dream then
that she awakes to find he is there,
sitting by her side, love shining in his eyes.

A DANCER WAITS FOR THE
INSIDE PLUNGE

Seek if you must, those wild women
who dance, hot in the night,
with long dancer's legs
that wrap around your driving need.
But do not tell me then, you hunger for love,
for I will ask you what this love is,
that you are speaking of.
Or do you believe all women
mistake love for sex.
You always tell me, I'm not like other women.
And if that is a criticism, it does not sting,
for I will be myself, and like no other,
and do not give a damn, if I am not as beautiful
or as young as the most recent soft creature
who catches your gaze.
I can dance alone and do not want a man
who sees only what he can touch, sink inside.
You say that you love me. Well then,
I must ask for your definition.
Does this shock you,

that a woman wants to define and explore
the connotations, and expectations
in your mind.
You say a man only wants to come inside.
But then such a man is no different
From all the others who sniff about
like dogs after a female in heat.
You fail to take the inner plunge
of the heart and mind.
Oh, go find yourself some other woman,
one wild enough to throw herself
into the dancing wind.
I would not scatter my soul to the wind
for you, or any other, and do not need you
to find true love –
the universe is so full –
I can simply close my eyes and ask,
believing that with enough trust,
what I seek,
a dance partner to take that inside plunge,
I shall find.

THE GODDESS

He who sings of the lover lost, forever
repeating the same refrain, is bound to repeat
the pattern, again, again, and again.
When did the song come to mean more than
the love it mourns, and how, in such a man,
can a new love ever be born?
She'll live forever in his eyes,
like those who die too young,
until soon she is only a penciled sketch
where once she was alive, full bodied
and warm.
He'll carve her out of marble, center her
in his garden's fountain of youth,
where she never grows old,
as he worships her over and over, wondering
why her heart was cold.

BUILD THE BED SOFT

She told him, build the bed soft, cover it
with silken pillows.
She did not know his silk would be soft enough
for comforting sleep and soul sighs, while
strong and steady, rhythmic as the ocean tide.
Deep enough to shelter her from raging storms
outside, as they, entwined, shared thoughts,
feelings, love, beyond space and time.
She told him build the bed soft, cover it
with silken pillows.
She did not know his bed was ready, because
he'd been building it all his life, waiting for one
who would fit perfectly upon his pillow.
She told him build the bed soft, cover it
with silken pillows.
She did not know his heart would be her pillow.

TRACINGS

His words leave traces, indelible ink,
across her skin, an invisible tattoo,
marking her as his. The memory will hold her,
when his arms cannot,
and even the thunderstorm outside,
could never wash away the pattern now traced
in her sands.
She waits in the dark. Lightning crashes,
thunder rolling, the boom loud, drowning out
all other sound, yet his words tap, tap, tap,
on the window of her mind. She dreams
of him.
Even without the photo, she would have
known. His eyes are kind, his smile gentler,
for her.
The other women do not matter.
She will not ask him to choose,
or place strings about his heart.
She gives herself, asks nothing in return.
Not even the smallest, of assurances.

She doesn't know how to love in half measures.
Her heart sings of what is imprinted there,
in curves one could monitor,
and perhaps one day he will sense signs
transparent to all, but him,
then he might follow the track,
across a thousand miles, to where
her heart sings.
This thought makes her close her eyes,
a smile crossing her lips, as she begins to trace
the trail his words left behind.

VEIL DANCER

His words reach her, teaching her things
about herself. She reads a line,
and closes her eyes, whispering yes,
before his words drive her to pen and paper.
She dances around the truth, spilling words
out onto the page. Words dangerous if spoken.
She never learned the dance of courtship,
and how the art of flirting can puzzle a woman
who never learned to love in half measures.
Like a foreign language, or a fine champagne,
it tickles the tongue. People claim it's harmless,
and that a sip won't hurt.
She finishes her message, sends it on its way,
hoping he will come to watch her dance today.
She has forgotten the story told long ago,
of a sultan who discovered a dancer,
and then claimed her for his own.
The dancer never saw her family again
and the rest of her life,
she danced only for men.

There was a secret dance, passed down
from woman to woman, the dance feeding
a passion which coils inside, unknown, while
the woman who learns to uncoil
is never the same.
As she dances past the tables, a memory
of the story suddenly returns to her again,
reminding her to be careful, around men.
No man has seen the dance of the uncoiling.
She will not dance it for him.
Now wrapped in veils she dances far enough
from the men
as her silk veil tangles n the wind.
He moves to her, and reaching out,
would pull the veil away,
if she danced near enough to touch.
She will remain
behind the veils she loves so much.

TAUNT

Her dreams taunt her in the daylight,
as logic and practicality battle what she feels
and hears whispered in her visions in the night.
What seemed so real, now fled, leaving her
with need and the empty bed.
She wipes the sand from her eyes.
A splash of cold water on her face, the shock
no less a surprise,
compared to what her mind won't grasp
of the dreams which drive away her past.
And yet, upon waking, that ghost
haunts her still, taunting - what will you do, silly girl, upon
waking to live, in the real world -
(And such a world is good at crushing dreams.)
The other ghost chimes in - your shadow world is nothing
like it seems.
The fairytale does not exist -
yet she foolishly insists, on chasing through the foggy mist,
to blindly follow her heart,
as the fog of desire drifts, up and over,

through the open window, the silver moon
spinning a song this dancer cannot resist.
For this is her song, their song,
carried by his voice on the wind,
as he sings what is only written in his heart.
And she knows one day,
she will follow that tune,
across field, meadow, mountain, sea, and dune,
for she simply cannot keep away.
And in her dreams, he waits, with open arms
and a smile so wide,
she can't help but hold this image, deep inside.
And as the ghostly taunts rise to a roar,
she closes her eyes, and says, "Spirits,
plague me no more."

EMERGING FROM THE DESERT

She emerged from the desert. He stood,
waiting, water dipper in hand,
and if he waited for her,
or offered the same gift to everyone,
she did not question the way women do
who want to be special.
She knew only that she was thirsty,
and too close to death. She drank
and closed her eyes,
thinking he must be an angel.
Surely this meant
she had come to a beautiful place to live.
He took her hand, proved he was solid enough, as he led her
into the tent, where she might rest. But she could never rest
at night.
Secrets she thought would keep her whole, have torn her
apart, as dreams haunted her.
The pen and paper by the bed tempting,
she begins to write, releasing secrets, slowly
seeping out, the vein severed, blood flowing

into the inkwell.
Her pen now dripping tainted, venomous echoes
across the page, sending up a vapor
with each memory traced.
She tries not to breathe in the fumes.
And he is wise to handle the pages carefully.
Parched, she cups his words in her hands,
drinks them in like water, as only a woman
emerged from the desert may drink.
If she cries easily now, tears tumbling
down her cheeks,
it is only because her tears are no longer dry,
and she, no longer hides so he won't see them.
Sometimes a whiff of vapor causes
doubt to rise, that invisible snake coiling
as confusion.
Then questions tumble from dry lips.
He offers her the next sip of water
and understanding.
She is not herself in those moments,
and if this pains him, he is unwavering.
He sees how she suffers from the poison
and knows he must wait until she is cleansed.
Within the darkened tent of their belonging,
a candle glows in the dark night.
Steadily burning it whispers, this is,
and though she does not name it,
she sees the flame, even with her eyes closed,
as she drifts off to sleep, it's flickering
the one constant, in her dreams.

DANCE PARTNERS

DANCE PARTNER

We once went dancing every Friday night.
One week Scottish Country Dance, the next
Contra. But we haven't been back,
since his death, as he likes to call it.
It's been two years now.
I couldn't go without him,
though he said I should.
I didn't want to answer questions,
didn't want to say,
my husband doesn't want to dance with me,
since he flatlined for three minutes,
and though they brought him back,
somehow the dance partner part of him
must have been left on the other side.
I am my own dance partner now,
and have belly dance sisters,
who are always ready to dance with abandon,
as I play the zills.
We used to say to each other,
it doesn't matter who you dance with,

but who you go home with, that matters.
I've had many dance partners from whom
I've walked away.
When we took a cruise, I stayed in the disco,
dancing, while he headed to bed,
because I'm a night owl
and can't stand to miss out on dancing,
while he's the early bird.
Life is short and I made a vow
to myself,
to never stand on the sidelines,
longing to dance,
and so, I keep it.

ADAGIO

She did not learn to dance
when she was young.
Watching the other children play,
crossing one awkward leg beneath her skirt,
to hide her clunky shoes, she would lean back
against the old oak tree, which hid her
from the bully, as she escaped
into the world of her book,
where she could be anything,
and magic happened even to ugly ducklings.
One night in her dreams, many years after
all these things had been forgotten,
he simply arrived, smiled at her,
and held out his hand.
She paused only briefly,
before placing her hand in his, with a smile
that lit up the night sky,
making the stars laugh,
as he led her onto the largest cloud.
Of course, by then she had grown,

into a swanish woman, with long shapely legs,
her memories the only remnant left behind.
And perhaps her treatment was like a ballet.
Each step prearranged to engineer a situation
of perfection and beauty –
perfection reached,
with no small amount of pain.
So, though she had never learned the first step
of ballet, like the other girls,
She still understood elements of the dance –
How to arabesque is to balance
and the Pas de deux requires collaboration,
between two strong individuals.
When they reached the center of the cloud,
he spoke one word – "Adagio" –
and she caught her breath.
Before the orchestra even began, she knew,
that though she did not have the skill,
she had the strength,
which comes from enduring much,
and her heart whispered, yes, I will trust,
as her soul did a pirouette of joy.

OUR SONG

The day our son's finance asked
if we had a song, to dance to at their wedding,
my mind went blank. We'd never had a song
that was ours, so, I picked one for us
to dance to at the wedding.
As we stepped onto that dance floor,
and the music began, I asked him
if he knew this song, 'Sailing', one of my favorites,
and he nodded yes.
As we danced, I was reminded
of how every Friday night,
when our sons were older, we would go out
dancing, one week Scottish Country Dance,
the next Contra dance,
and of high school dances when we were dating.
I would never have dated a boy
who would not dance with me,
and we both enjoyed dancing with each other,
so, puzzled, I asked
how we could be married so long

without ever having a song that was ours.
He said, he guessed he wasn't that into music.
Our song on this night 'Sailing', I chose
because it reminds me of our catamaran
in Bora Bora, skimming across the ocean,
sting rays racing beneath the two of us,
as he worked the sails,
and the open sky.
Fantasy does get the best of me
when I'm sailing, and some nights
I need a little fantasy of sailing away,
which is where I am, for one brief dance,
thinking of that open sky.

MAKING LOVE

Making love, we dance as one, yet two,
beneath this moon -
Once two stars did collide
into starlight powder, a dusty milky way
of thighs, entwined, like your heart and mine.
Your voice whispered, that echo
awakened my soul's joy, a quick glimmer
of joy to come, when the broken is at last
made whole, to begin anew,
and with your kisses showering down,
I drink them in, breathe deep, and then,
give them back again.
Oh, wrap my limbs, my life, within
your loving arms, and wipe away these tears,
for all those years are gone,
and I promise not to turn, over my shoulder,
to look back at ghosts waiting to haunt.
No, I will keep my focus clearly, with you,
my focal point on what is true.
For yesterday is gone, and the hands of time

sweep all away -
even our mistakes,
and tomorrow will never come.
(She is a fickle guest, making those promises
in her sweet way, but she will never dance
with us.)
Today we live forever, in this moment,
which is all we have, to breathe in love,
giving life to one another,
while breathing that breath of love,
back out again.
A different kind of dance.
How could we have known,
what we were missing so long ago,
when our hearts were whispering
silent prayers
in the dark.

BATHING

She sinks, warm water up to her chin,
eyes drifting closed, inhales the calming scent
of lavender, and feels the invisible traces,
of dry tears down her cheeks.
She senses warmth radiating, filling the room
with a presence so strong, she knows, before
ever opening her eyes, rock-steady he awaits, with tender-
ness and eyes so kind.
She draws a breath, forbids herself to tremble.
He kneels. His fingers trace down her temple,
a soft brush stroke, tracing a line of cheekbone
and jaw.
She cannot help but close her eyes again.
"It's okay," he murmurs, his voice wrapping
around her like velvet.
His hand closes over hers. Warm strong fingers,
gently removing the washcloth.
Nimbly he smooths it across her cheeks.
A caress to wipe away tears. And at his tender
touch, she inhales, counts to three,

not sure she isn't dreaming.
She manages a tremulous smile,
and he is still there when her eyes open,
which leads her to believe, he isn't going
anywhere.
"It's okay," he murmurs, his face mingling an
eager tenderness, as his eyes bathe her.
He runs the cloth up her neck, his words
running through her mind.
She arches her head back, sighs.
The soapy cloth slides down,
across her breasts, ivory hills now flushed
to darker peaks where his eyes linger.
Rivulets run down the valley,
between right and left. He lifts her foot,
washing each toe in turn,
the little toe she broke once,
the ankle that flares, dance exacting a toll.
The black mark atop her foot,
where a pencil once drove in.
She is no cover model.
There are too many small imperfections.
"It's okay," he murmurs as his eyes exclaim
how beautiful she is, to him.
His hand moves up her leg, slowing washing
from ankle to calf, then up her thigh.
She tenses slightly, wonders
if he'll keep moving up.
'It's okay, 'he murmurs, as he stops
to move on to her other foot,
where he begins the pattern again.
Warmth gathers inside her. Trust rewarded.
The cloth moves over her rounded belly,

his fingers splayed, as water pools in her
navel.
"Sit up," he says, "I'll wash your hair."
Fingertips ease over her scalp, clearing away
tension, chasing thoughts.
Careful to keep soap out of her eyes, his fingers
move in circles. Slippery hair slides through his
fingers.
"Keep your eyes closed now," he says, as he
cups his hands, carries water up to rinse her,
again, and again. A trickling waterfall.
Small streams running over flushed skin.
"It's okay," he murmurs, "It's safe to open your
eyes."
He holds out his hands, and
placing her hands in his, she trusts.
Their eyes meet and hold, before he guides her
one small step, up and over and then another
until she stands before him, his eyes washing
over her body. She shivers slightly.
"It's okay," he murmurs, releasing her hands
to reach for the towel. He wraps the towel
around her, his eyes never leaving,
which tells her he would do so much more.
He tucks the towel together, then gives it to her
to hold. Hers the choice to keep it there,
or let it drop.
The small move stokes overwrought nerves,
like a tonic. His warm hands gather up her wet,
tousled hair, to blot drenched coils in a towel,
then his fingers rake through, dividing
wet strands, to tumble down her back.
"It's okay," he murmurs as he tosses away

the soaked towel, and his plans for the evening.
Gathering her into his arms,
he stands behind her, arms wrapped around her,
he gives her a squeeze, his arms warm..
"It's okay," he says, kissing the top of her head.
She quivers, a long spasm of release, relaxing a
screaming tension, to rest secure in his arms.
He will hold her, for as long as she needs.

I CANNOT SLEEP

"If we dreamt the same thing every night, it would affect us as much as the objects we see every day." -Pascal

I cannot sleep, for when I do,
my dreams keep returning to you –
The shadow man
who dances me across the sky.
Was it in a dream he woke my soul,
so it might fly –
and oh, how far we have flown,
the shadow man and I,
The settings of these dreams vary so,
the only recurring theme I see
is the shadow man I know, yet do not know.
Oh, all these crazy dreams must stop, because
I need to sleep.
Dark circles spread beneath my eyes, so deep.
And this I fear - trusting in dreams,
as things are seldom what they seem.
These visions are not crystal clear,

and my shadow man, neither are you.
I cannot see to tell what is true, but this I know -
the more you visit me each night,
the more I think of you.
There is a battle waging here,
between dark beautiful night
and bright dangerous day.
The sounds of battle are so loud,
I cannot find my way.
My waking self and my sleeping self
are now constantly in debate.
The subject-
if there is such a thing as fate.

AFTER THE SUN SETS - BEFORE THE FINAL CURTAIN

USED COWS FOR SALE

Used Cows for Sale,
the sign on the highway reads,
And I think of all the stories and poems
I've read and listened to at this week's
Antioch writers workshop -
so many tales of the divorced,
and how milk flows from mothers,
their bodies growing heavy, as slowly
they forget how their lithe bodies would dance,
once upon a time, before children.
And who wants a used cow, I wonder.
In our country, we want everything
fresh and new,
yet I have known women who aged
so beautifully, as if to make it an art.
Which is why I will never see myself
as some old cow, standing around in a pasture,
waiting for a new owner to place value on me,
because my current owner has lost interest.
No, no, I do not wish to be owned,

nor will I stand in some damn field.
Now that the children are grown -
I'll dance and spin.
No fence is tall enough to keep me in,
and though I cannot tell you
where I might go,
there was a tale I heard once, long ago -
of a cow who jumped over the moon.

CLIMBING TOGETHER

And as his loving fingers seek mine,
before we climb, threading through
to hold them close, my heart sings yes,
he loves you,
despite your weary smile and wounded heart,
tired dancer that you are, he loves you true,
and neither time, nor fate, nor death,
can take one bit of this away from you.
So do not fear this hike –
Love is not love which does not last,
beyond the harshest paths of life –
Love will survive if deep and true,
and strong as it is,
it makes us but the stronger too,
for it will draw us close, even as it hurts,
but hurting, then requires
a tending tenderness.
And love which is never easy, ever tests us thus,
that we might be kind and patient,
teaching us to trust.

Love bears all tests, and even more, bears time.
And yet we run from pain, to hide,
not wishing to carry such things inside,
that would make us cry and question –
why the paths are never straight,
the obstacles between two hearts,
so rocky with such steep inclines,
they leave us winded.
The moment we reach that mountaintop,
I'll long for nothing but your hand,
once again, in mine

QUIETUDE

The house is quiet now,
and I have finally learned to love the silence.
No longer twirling here and there, fast as I can,
shimmying the frenzy of the troubled,
or those who avoid things.
The only sound is the clock ticking, while
even the ghosts of the past are silent now.
This house breathes deep,
waits with open arms, seeking nothing,
and I am told I laugh now, in my sleep.
Somewhere inside of me lives a still pond,
a calm center, and when I close my eyes,
I can almost see the brook giggling,
while fireflies dance in the air,
and oh, how that song of mating
makes me smile, for I know
that wherever I go upon this wide earth,
I carry it with me.
If you could look into my eyes,
you might see this place reflected,

though for the friend who asked
if I was stoned, I'll only shake my head
and smile.
For some, the secrets are best kept inside.
They must find their center on their own.
All I can say is this - I feel a deep peace,
and no longer search to fill those empty places.
The cave, which lives by the sea, knows
how the ebb and flow, both fills and empties,
waits patiently, and rejoices in the fullness
of both sea and air,
for a glass can be half full and be half empty.
We are taught to look for what we lack.
Yet even an empty space may hold something,
unseen.
And if we do not learn to love
our empty places...
Well, one can shout into the cave, yet only hear
the echo of the shouting,
and who can think with all that chatter?
How long can you sit in silence,
before turning on the radio?
And why are we so afraid
of listening to ourselves?
To be alone is not necessarily to be lonely.
I do not mind if the phone does not ring,
or no one comes to knock on my door.
Though I would answer with joy,
if you were on the other side.
Tonight, when I thought of you,
I closed my eyes and smiled –
And if I could tell you only one thing,
it would be this –

I find I'm smiling all the time now,
at the smallest of things,
as if I were a young child.
Perhaps if you were to close your eyes
and listen very closely,
you might hear in the distance,
the giggle of the brook, the heart,
the inner child.

ONE SMALL CHIME

In the distance I hear him singing,
and something within him,
touches something within me.
Like a bell ringing, or one small chime,
which resonates deep within my soul.
A whispered yes on the wind,
which if it carries strong and true,
might carry back to him.
And this, this which we do not name,
is with me as I wake or sleep, and I wonder
if somewhere on another plane, our souls dance,
unrestricted by time or space
hearts and hands, entwined, for all time,
to the constant low ringing of one small chime.

ELEMENTAL

It is incomprehensible to me, the pattern
of our dance.
The underlying beat. The flowing over or under.
The lure of a heart beating so strong,
tender eyes, that kindness, a pattern of a poem
yet to be written across the night sky.
And ungraspable flashes of understanding
which crackled with the lightning,
of two creative minds, the hurricane's eye,
when all is briefly clear. For the moment of yes,
a slow dance, inside four corners,
a quiet cave, which deadens wind.
In that moment we live forever,
time waits, and even the sands stand still,
to repeat a whispered yes.

FOR YOU

For you, my love,
I will dance,
in the spirit of the night,
where we are unbound
by what is right,
and time and distance
hold no place,
beyond the moon and stars,
I cup your face,
stretch up to kiss your lips -
my soul does sing, of this
and many things ...
I dance for you,
beneath the sheets,
I dream of you, my love,
in the dark of night.

MUDDLED AFTER THE STROKE

Being foggy, this newly muddled brain
won't jump quick, to leap in, to double Dutch
inside the jump rope of communication,
and then twirl around to the other side
with a laugh.
Even a single jump rope trips me these days,
and I miss the lightness, the leap
of the quick reaction, the old connection
instantaneous as I followed your words,
connotations and allusions crashing
like cymbals in my mind, shouting yes,
as we would leap across mountains and seas,
to dance.

I wonder how it is for you, on the other side
of this fog -
If you grow frustrated at my inability
to hear you clearly, or tire of having to
repeat yourself, in my right ear, as the left
got left behind somewhere during the stroke,

and if you are still waiting for me
to make that old leap again, when instead
I offer confusion,
and if perhaps you cannot help but wonder,
if I've understood what you're saying,
or if you wonder where the rest of me is,
lost in that fogginess,
that old part of me out there somewhere,
looking for your hand.

MOONSHINE

The story is old, ancient as the moon,
commanding from the sky, directing
the stars to shine,
the dew to glisten across the lawn,
each blade of grass to echo
that whisper which will entrance,
and as it does, she will dance.
On and on she goes, tripping across
with dew dampened toes.
She believes she is flinging away bits of the past,
says the day is too harsh, as watching the moon, she is
entranced, to believe a dream
is what is real.
But none of this is true.
You know how a dream can seem real.
It's the story of the moment you pinch yourself,
to see if you are really feeling what you feel.
It's a story I may tell you one day,
while grandchildren chase each other
across the lawn, and play, as crickets chirp,

and the silver moon comes out again,
to shine upon our silvered hairs.
Perhaps then I will reach for your hand,
and thread my fingers through yours,
to tug you away from the rocking chair,
which creaks, as surely as old bones.
And if the moon is then kind,
a woman will dance again,
across the silvered lawn,
forgetting all sense and time,
once again young and beautiful, in your eyes,
while the moonlight shines.

ACKNOWLEDGMENTS

To all the women who have come into my life through dance, and who have shared their stories with me in some way, thank you. The braiding of these memories could not have been woven into these poems without you.

Thank you to all my dance instructors for some of the most wonderful years of my life and for sharing your joy in the dance along with your skills. I treasure those memories.

Thank you to my husband for putting the dance room in our home with mirrors on two walls for rehearsing and teaching dance, for attending performances and taking pictures, for being supportive of my work for Shimmy Mob, and for being my dance partner from the time I was sixteen on our first dates, to asking me for that slow dance after the stroke last year. For supporting my writing all of these years.

Thank you to my critique group, Valentina Taran and Steve Black for critiquing many of my poems.

Thank you to every reader who discovered one or more of my poems on MySpace when so many poets were there posting and who left comments of encouragement for my work. I read every single one.

Thank you to my cover artist Sheri L. McGathy, who has created so many wonderful covers for me for my fiction. For this poetry collection of dance poems, we used pictures from my dance years and she worked her magic to make my selections work.

Special thanks to my best friend, Valentina Taran, first

reader for this collection, and the editor of my first poetry collection, Twilight Dips.

For years she has encouraged me to publish more of my poems and to share them with the world.

Infinite love and gratitude to you all.

DEBRA THE DANCER

As a child, Debra Bishop did not dance.

She wore corrective shoes with metal plates during her elementary school years. Dance entered her life when she was a teenager attending school dances, and finally as an adult, she took her first dance classes.

Dance to Debra, has always meant freedom.

Belly dance wasn't her first dance form, though it stayed with her the longest. Prior to belly dancing, Debra and her husband danced with the Memphis Scottish Country Dancers and with a Contra Dance group on weekends. One day, her husband decided he no longer wanted to attend.

Soon after, Debra attended Shadowcon, a Memphis, TN event. A free bellydance class put on by Desert Rose dancers was taught in a hafla suite which held decorations and middle eastern foods. She fell in love with the dance, was fascinated by the history, music, stories, and coin belts. She didn't need a partner, and could dance with other women in a social group.

She continued studying different styles, and one year was the only dancer in Memphis to perform at student shows with three different studios. Though urged by her instructors to pick one (of course theirs), that wasn't what she wanted. As a Gemini, (she shares a birthday with Prince) Debra has always had multiple interests, and wanted to learn every form of the dance that she could.

Eventually, she had to choose, and as she was one of the founding members of Shakti Global Fusion, she agreed to go on troupe contract, and to perform and teach. Taking the dance name Shai'ra Rakisa, she danced professionally. Sha'ira is the feminine form of Sha'ir (Arabic poet) Rakisa meaning dancer.

Debra has always been a poet and writer. The years when she danced every day were some of her most prolific. Dancing seven days a week, there was a year when she wrote a poem every single day. One creative endeavor fed the other.

With her first novel coming out in 2008, Debra left the troupe, retired, and traded performances for book signings. She would soon be dancing with words.

Debra's active dance years:

2005- 2007 -with Desert Rose Dance
    2007 - with Memphis Raqs
    2007 - 2008 troupe member Shakti Global Fusion Belly Dance
    2008 – retired from dancing
    2009 - Desert Rose Dance performance as alumni
    2011 – came out of retirement to found Shimmy Mob Memphis on March 28th raising funds for the local domestic abuse shelter in Memphis which was a refuge for women

and children from three states. International Shimmy Mob bestowed honors on Team Leader on Debra and her two assistants, Brenda Canady, and Cymbeline Rois, and honored the entire Memphis team this year.

2012 – Shimmy Mob Memphis Team Leader

2013 – Shimmy Mob Memphis Asst. Team Leader

2014 – Shimmy Mob Memphis Asst. Team Leader

2015 - Shimmy Mob Memphis Asst. Team Leader

2016 –Shimmy Mob Memphis -broken foot, sat out

2017 – Shimmy Mob Memphis Dancer

2018 –Shimmy Mob Memphis - health issue/out

2019 – Shimmy Mob Durham, NC Dancer

2020 – Shimmy Mob Durham, NC Dancer

2021 – Shimmy Mob Durham, NC Dancer

Debra and her husband sold their home just outside Memphis in 2020 and moved into a 43 foot motorhome to live full time and travel the U.S.A.

Debra has studied many different belly dance styles. Beginning with Cabaret, classical Egyptian and folkloric styles taught by *Zeina, (Dee Birnbaum)* Memphis, TN private instructor at Rhodes college, and at Desert Rose Dance.

Drawn to the cultural, historic and folkloric aspects of the dances from each country, Debra could not have had a better first teacher.

One of her best memories was modeling clothing from Zeina's collection, which is now preserved here: https://iumaa.iu.edu/collections/ethnographic-collections/birnbaum.html

Another article about the collection. https://news.rhodes.edu/stories/piece-middle-east-heart-memphis

Debra's favorite dance studying under Zeina was the

fortune teller dance, where she learned to play zills (finger cymbals) for the first time, something she quickly loved.

Debra added classes in Classical Egyptian and Cabaret with Feyrouz at Desert Rose Dance and with studio owner, Samra, and joined the student performance group, performing for the first time. Shy at first, Samra had to talk her into performing. She had so much fun dancing with the other women the first time that she learned to love performing.

Branching out into Tribal bellydance styles while also at Desert Rose, she took classes with Juli Downum (urban tribal belly dance) of Chattanooga's Dandasha; and Liz (tribal fusion) of Memphis Raqs, where she was a member of the student performance group.

Her favorite class during this period was Turkish Rom (not gypsy, they prefer to be called Rom) taught by Elizabeth Strong of Ultra Gypsy, and Belly dance Superstars. https://strongdancer.com/biography/

Turkish Rom is still one of Debra's favorites to dance and to watch.

After taking a global fusion class with Asha Devi, at Shadowcon, she was invited to be a founding member of Shakti Global Fusion, in Memphis.

At a Belly dance Superstars weekend in Nashville, TN, Debra took classes with Rachel Brice, (tribal and yoga) https://www.rachelbrice.com/ with Jillina, https://www.jillina.com/ and drumming, zills and Arabic rhythms with master percussionist Issam Houshan https://www.tablabyissam.com/

She took every class possible, wanting to learn as much as she could. This was her way even after she was a troupe dancer on contract. She wanted to keep learning more.

She learned to perform to a live drum, improv, and to drum with Wils Crater drummer for Shakti Global Fusion.

Shakti troupe took a class with Ariella (dark fusion belly dance) https://www.ariellah.com/ and performed at the Black Hearts Ball. This was their only performance away from Memphis, TN.

On her own, Debra continued taking classes with Mira Betts, GA (tribal) http://miramania.com/; Shahira Raqs; Madrina, Tampa, FL (Egyptian Raqs Sharki) https://www.madrinhadances.com/; Amani Jabril, Atlanta, GA (folkloric Khaleghi) https://www.theamanijabril.com/about; Sadiia Lamm, Pyramid Dance, Memphis, TN (hula) https://www.facebook.com/sadiia.lamm; Isadora Bukowski (La Tejedora) https://orientaldancer.net/belly-dance-library/belly-dance-competitions/tribal-belly-dance-idol-feature.php ; and the wonderful Leila Gamal.

In 2010 Debra came out of retirement to take a class from Mahoumed Reda, choreographer and founder of world-famous Reda troupe, (classical Egyptian)

https://en.wikipedia.org/wiki/Mahmoud_Reda

In 2011 she came out of retirement once more, to join Shimmy Mob's international event which raises funds and awareness for local domestic abuse shelters. www.shimmy-mob.com

It is said, "Once a dancer, always a dancer." Debra was always ready to learn a new dance and to step up, for Shimmy Mob, and the local shelter. Each year on international belly dance day, when dancers all around the world, wearing the same t-shirts, performing the same choreography to the same song to raise funds for local shelters, dancing with the group gave her goose bumps. To Debra, this is the true meaning of sisterhood. Love in action.

"Dance can unite us all. We don't have to speak the same language." – Debra Parmley

In her travels, Debra has witnessed Tahitian and fire dances on the islands of Tahiti, and Bora Bora, belly dance and Rom dance in Turkey, Greek dancing in Greece, and Scottish dancing in Scotland.

In late June 2023, Debra had a stroke in the balance section of her brain, which caused her to have balance issues, to need a walker to walk, and she cannot drive. She waits for new neural pathways to form and hopes to one day be able to dance freely again. Until then, she dances in her heart, savors her memories and dances with words.

To celebrate her 62nd birthday on June 7th, 2024, she released this collection of 61 poems, most of them pulled from her active dance years.

This collection is a gift to herself, to her dance sisters and to her friends and family.

DEBRA THE AUTHOR

Author Debra Parmley believes "Every day we are alive is a beautiful day." She likes to give her readers and her story people a story that ends happily.

An Air Force veteran's wife, Debra writes suspense/thriller, military romantic suspense, contemporary military romance, historical romance, urban fantasy romance, fairy tale romance, holiday romance, poetry, and memoir.

Debra married her high school sweetheart, whom she asked out after a five-dollar bet. After living in five states with her husband and their two sons, and then living 23 years just outside Memphis, TN, she and her husband sold everything in 2020 and now live and travel the U.S. in their 43-foot motorhome full-time.

Debra is an adventurous writer who has climbed lighthouses because she is afraid of heights.

She worked as an independent travel agent and has set foot in more than 13 countries. She has walked the plank of a pirate ship off the coast of Grand Cayman, gone swimming with dolphins in Moorea, French Polynesia, and escorted a bus full of clients through Scotland.

Disabled in July, 2023, after a stroke, through she can no longer drive, she continues to enjoy living and traveling in their motorhome.

You can read about her travels on her Beautiful Day Traveler blog https://beautifuldaytraveler.wordpress.com/

Debra's Beautiful Day YouTube Channel:
youtube.com/channel/UC27hTWse4gLJxTETQw6i7xw/
for travel videos, for videos of Debra reading first chapters from her books, for Wednesday Words with Debra, and chats about her RV lifestyle and writing.

Visit www.debraparmley.com

As Debra Bishop, she writes fairy tales, fantasy, and children's books.

Coming soon: https://debrabishop.com/

ALSO BY DEBRA PARMLEY

POETRY:

Twilight Dips: poetry collection – Debra's early poems- eBook, paperback

Everything Begins in the Belly: poetry collection - eBook, paperback June 7, 2024

MILITARY ROMANTIC SUSPENSE:

Green Brotherhood SEAL Team XII series:

Finding Bryce, book one - eBook, paperback

Real Movie Hero, book two - eBook, paperback

Saving the Bellydancer, book three - eBook, paperback

Green Brotherhood Trilogy #1 - eBook boxset, paperback

Brotherhood Protectors series:

Montana Marine - book one - eBook, paperback

Defensive Instructor - book two -eBook, paperback

Marine Protector - book three- eBook, paperback

Marine Protectors - box set - eBook.

Blind Trust - book four - eBook, paperback

A Triple C Ranch Christmas Wedding - book five - eBook, paperback

Montana Delta Rescue - book six - eBook, paperback

Montana SEAL Protector - book seven - eBook, paperback

Montana Rodeo Protector - book eight - 2024

∼

Bobbins Sisters Trilogy:

Check Out – book one, eBook, paperback.

Check In – book two, eBook, paperback.

Check Mate – book three - 2024.

∼

Single Title Contemporary:

Aboard the Wishing Star - eBook, paperback

∼

SUSPENSE -THRILLER – with Romance:

To Catch an Elf – eBook, paperback, Large Print Hardcover

∼

URBAN FANTASY ROMANCE:

Vague Directions: Into the Woods - eBook, paperback.

∼

WESTERN HISTORICAL ROMANCE:

Gone to Texas: A Desperate Journey - (original sweeter version) - Large Print Hardcover, eBook, paperback.

Dangerous Ties - eBook, paperback

Deadly Adversaries - eBook, paperback

Desperate, Dangerous, Deadly: A Western Collection – eBook box set

Isabella, Bride of Ohio: American Mail Order Bride – (original sweeter version) - Large Print Hardcover, eBook, paperback

Penny From Deadwood - 2024

1920's ROMANCE:

Butterflies Fly Free series:

Trapping the Butterfly – book one, eBook, paperback, Large Print Hardcover

Dancing Butterfly – book two, eBook, paperback

Exotic Butterfly – book three, Nov. 2024

HOLIDAY ROMANCE:

Jenna's Christmas Wish – eBook, paperback

The Twelve Stitches of Christmas – fairy tale short story

DYSTOPIAN ROMANCE:

The Hunger Roads Trilogy:

Another Change of Scenery – Aug. 2024

Down a Back Road – 2024

Into the Convergence Zone – 2024

NONFICTION:

Anywhere But Here: Our First Year Full Time RV Living on the Road – 2024

Out of Print:

Protecting Pippa

Split Screen Scream

Protecting Zarifah

Vague Directions – short story

A Desperate Journey

Isabella, Bride of Ohio

Tales of Deadwood - anthology

We Know the Truth, Do You? Area 51 – anthology (going to the moon/time capsule)

Wounded Heroes - anthology

Hansel & Gretel: Down the Rabbit Hole – anthology

More Monsters from Memphis – anthology

WRITING AS DEBRA BISHOP:

Fairytales for all ages:

The Sweetest Day - Hansel and Gretel fairytale - eBook, paperback

YA:

The Rolling House – time travel 2024

Children's:

coming in 2024.